CLOUD SECURITY ESSENTIALS

Security Architecture Series for All Levels.

Tim Coakley

TABLE OF CONTENTS

PREFACE

Welcome to this critical area within cybersecurity, cloud security. This book is designed to provide you with the necessary information needed to navigate the ever-evolving challenges of protecting data, applications, and infrastructure in the cloud.

As organisations increasingly rely on technology to undertake their business needs, the vulnerabilities within these systems become a target of opportunity for malicious actors. Ensuring the security of cloud solutions, whether they are software applications, hardware devices, or integrated systems, has become necessary to safeguarding people, data, privacy, and the integrity of our growing global digital infrastructure.

Cloud security requires a multi-dimensional approach that includes identifying potential security threats, implementing protective or detective security measures, and applying continuous monitoring while meeting user and business needs. Cloud security extends across various security domains, which include data protection, access control, security operations, and risk management. A consistent cloud security strategy not only defends against external threats but also mitigates and reduces internal risks, human errors, and the growing global legal and compliance challenges faced by businesses.

In the last decade alone, advancements have been made in key technology areas such as processing speeds, mobile computing, the Internet of Things (IoT), automation, and artificial intelligence. These technologies are reshaping both how we work and the pace of change, driving the need for a more proactive and extensive way to perform cloud security. Having strong cloud security in place builds trust with customers, business partners, and solution stakeholders, giving a level of assurance that their information and interactions with solutions are safe and secure.

Everyday individuals, organisations, and even nation states face an ever-growing array of cyber threats, ranging from phishing attempts to sophisticated nation-state-sponsored attacks. The need for skilled professionals who can safeguard our cloud infrastructure has never been greater. This book is designed to help you move in the right direction, equipping you with more knowledge and a greater understanding of cloud security.

In this book, we aim to cover the field of cybersecurity as it applies to cloud services used within a business setting. We will equip you with the fundamental concepts and principles necessary to defend against a wide range of cyber threats. Whether you're a student starting on a career in cloud security, a professional seeking to enhance your skills, or simply an individual interested in understanding the essentials of cloud security, this book is written to meet your needs.

We first begin by looking at defining some of the common high-level terms used. We then delve into the fundamental principles of cloud security. As we progress, we'll look at the various layers of defence, including logging and secure services.

Throughout the book, examples are provided to help reinforce your understanding and enable you to apply the concepts in the real world. After reading this book, you will have learned the knowledge and skills necessary to proactively identify and mitigate cyber threats specific to cloud security in a business context.

It is important to note that both cybersecurity and cloud security are ever-evolving fields, with new threats, ways of working, and technologies constantly emerging and being developed. While this book provides a solid foundation in the essentials, it is crucial to stay up to date and continue learning as the field develops. The learning never stops!

The hope is that this book sparks your curiosity, ignites your passion for all things cloud security and cybersecurity, and serves as a valuable resource on your journey to becoming an even more proficient cybersecurity professional.

ACKNOWLEDGEMENT

This book would not have been possible without the knowledge and experience learned from colleagues over the years up to current time within the cyber security industry. We all stand on the shoulders of giants to succeed, and this book is a testament to that fact.

INTRODUCTION

Are you new to cloud security or looking to expand your knowledge in this field? Whether you are just starting out or an experienced professional, this book aims to guide you through the complexities of cloud security.

Cloud security is not a new concept, but its importance is growing rapidly as businesses face increasing threats from insecure internet facing solutions. It is necessary to incorporate strong protections and multi-layered defences throughout the solution design, delivery, and operation phases. This must be done while managing constrained budgets, user needs, and fast-moving technologies. We will cover the basics of cloud security, and the information a security architect needs to know, and delve into the essentials of implementing security measures.

We will examine how human factors influence the use of cloud solutions and discuss the various stages of designing and building secure cloud infrastructures.

We will then explore different design perspectives, including designs and important cloud services. Understanding these services and their properties is crucial for ensuring the security and design of your cloud infrastructure.

Next, we will discuss data within a cloud solution, covering its creation, processing, and lifecycle. With various deployment models available, such as Infrastructure as a Service (IaaS) and Software as a Service (SaaS), there are numerous areas to protect as the attack surface increases. We will examine common components that make up a cloud solution and how security can be applied to each component.

By the end of this book, you will have an extensive understanding of cloud security and be equipped to implement strong security measures in your own cloud environments.

DISCLAIMER

The information provided in this book does not, and is not intended to, constitute legal advice, instead, all information, content, and materials available in this book are for general informational purposes only. Information in this book may not contain the most up to date legal or other information. This book contains some links to other third-party websites, these links are only for the convenience of the reader and nothing more.

WHAT IS CLOUD SECURITY

Before digging into the specifics, it is necessary to understand what cloud security entails. Cloud security encompasses the people, processes, and technologies used to protect cloud-based data, applications, and infrastructure from threats, known vulnerabilities, and reduce overall security risk. This protection begins from the initial design phase, including design evolution, until the released cloud hosted solution, services and infrastructure are decommissioned and no longer required.

The primary threats to be guarded against include data breaches where a cloud solution is compromised and data is stolen, unauthorised access, and any other malicious acts, as defined by the laws and regulations of a particular country.

The goal of cloud security is to prevent or reduce the likelihood of threats and vulnerabilities becoming exploitable. This is achieved by building strong solutions that can withstand security threats. To accomplish this, it is crucial to understand all potential risks and then identify ways to mitigate these risks in advance, using the resources available as early as reasonably possible.

By adopting an extensive approach to cloud security, organisations can ensure the integrity and confidentiality of their data, applications, and infrastructure, thereby enhancing their overall security posture in the cloud.

FOUNDATIONS & FRAMEWORKS

The swift adoption of cloud computing has revolutionised organisational operations, offering unparalleled scalability, efficiency, and cost savings. However, these advantages are accompanied by substantial security challenges. Cloud security extends beyond merely protecting data; it encompasses safeguarding applications, networks, and infrastructure against a dynamically evolving threat environment.

This chapter provides a foundational understanding of cloud security, digging into its core principles, shared responsibility models, and the frameworks that guide best practices. Whether you are a novice or an experienced professional, understanding these fundamentals is necessary for constructing strong defences and fostering a "security first" culture in the cloud.

WHY CLOUD SECURITY IS IMPORTANT

In today's digital environment, cloud computing has become the foundation of innovation, offering unparalleled scalability, flexibility, and cost efficiency. However, as businesses increasingly migrate critical operations to the cloud, the importance of cloud security has never been greater. Securing cloud environments is crucial to safeguard sensitive data, ensure business continuity, and maintain customer trust.

Cloud environments introduce unique security challenges. Unlike traditional on-premises setups, cloud infrastructures are dynamic, distributed, and highly interconnected. These characteristics make them vulnerable to a range of threats, including data breaches, insider attacks, and misconfigurations. High-profile incidents, such as breaches caused by exposed databases or poorly managed access controls, highlight how even minor security lapses can lead to catastrophic consequences.

The shared responsibility model, which defines the roles of cloud providers and customers in securing the environment, adds another layer of complexity. Organisations must ensure they meet their part of the responsibilities, such as protecting their applications, data, and identity systems. Failure to do so can result in regulatory penalties, reputational damage, and financial losses.

Moreover, as cloud technologies develop, so do the threats. Adversaries exploit automation, machine learning, and new attack vectors, making proactive security measures necessary. Businesses must adopt a strong cloud security strategy that positions with their operational needs and compliance requirements.

CLOUD SECURITY MODELS

Cloud computing has significantly transformed how organisations deploy, manage, and scale their IT resources. The services are broadly categorised into three models: Infrastructure as a Service (IaaS), Platform as a Service (PaaS), and Software as a Service (SaaS). Each model offers unique features tailored to different business needs.

IaaS provides the foundational building blocks for IT infrastructure. It delivers virtualised computing resources such as virtual machines (VMs), storage, and networking on-demand. This model allows organisations to avoid the costs and complexities of managing physical servers. Providers like AWS, Azure, and Google Cloud offer scalability and flexibility, making IaaS ideal for businesses requiring high level of control over their environments.

PaaS abstracts the underlying infrastructure to provide a platform for application development and deployment. Developers can focus on coding without worrying about managing servers, operating systems, or middleware. PaaS solutions like Microsoft Azure App Service and Google App Engine are perfect for rapid application delivery, enabling more efficient integrations, and improving innovation.

SaaS delivers fully managed applications over the internet. Users access software like email, customer relationship management (CRM), and productivity tools directly via a web browser, eliminating the need for installation or maintenance. Examples include Microsoft 365, Salesforce, and Google Workspace.

Each cloud model positions with specific business goals, offering a range of customisation, scalability, and cost-efficiency. Choosing the right model depends on the organisation's requirements and technical expertise.

CLOUD SECURITY CHALLENGES

Cloud computing has revolutionised organisational operations, but it also introduces security challenges. Among the most critical are data breaches, misconfigurations, and insider threats, each posing unique risks to the integrity, confidentiality, and availability of cloud environments.

Data breaches remain one of the most concerning threats in cloud security. Attackers frequently target sensitive data stored in the cloud, such as customer information, intellectual property, and financial records. Weak encryption, insecure APIs, and credential theft are common routes for breaches. The consequences include regulatory penalties, reputational damage, and financial losses, underscoring the need for strong data protection strategies, with encryption and access controls.

Misconfigurations are a leading cause of cloud vulnerabilities. Open storage buckets, overly permissive access controls, and insecure network setups can expose critical resources to unauthorised access. These errors often occur due to the complexity of managing cloud environments and the lack of standardised security practices. Automating configuration management and leveraging Cloud Security Posture Management (CSPM) tools can help detect and prevent such issues.

Insider threats, whether malicious or accidental, are a growing concern in cloud environments. Employees, contractors, or partners with access to sensitive data can intentionally misuse their privileges or unintentionally compromise security through negligence. Organisations must implement zero-trust principles, monitor user activity, and conduct regular security training to mitigate these risks.

Addressing these challenges requires a proactive, layered approach to cloud security, ensuring that vulnerabilities are minimised, and threats are quickly mitigated.

CLOUD SECURITY MINDSET

In the context of digital transformation, adopting a security centric approach is no longer a choice, it is a necessity for protecting data, operations, and overall trust. A security centric approach prioritises protecting assets at every stage of development, deployment, and operation, so that security considerations are integral rather than an afterthought.

Cloud environments, while transformative, introduce unique challenges. The dynamic nature of cloud infrastructure, reliance on shared responsibility models, and increasing sophistication of cyber threats necessitate a proactive stance. A security-centric mindset ensures that organisations consistently anticipate and mitigate risks rather than reacting to breaches or failures.

One key benefit is the prevention of costly incidents. Data breaches, ransomware attacks, and misconfigurations can result in severe financial and reputational damage. By embedding security from the outset, organisations can reduce vulnerabilities, comply with regulations, and maintain customer trust.

A security-centric mindset also promotes a culture of accountability. It positions teams, developers, IT, and management around shared goals, ensuring that security practices are baked into daily operations and planning.

Combining teams like DevSecOps, which integrate security into development workflows, are an example of this shift, emphasizing continuous assessment and improvement.

As cyber threats develop, organisations that prioritise security are better positioned to adapt. They can embrace innovation, such as cloud native architectures, without compromising protection. Essentially, adopting a security-centric mindset is about ensuring resilience, safeguarding growth, and enabling trust in an increasingly digital world. Security isn't just a feature; but a fundamental business enabler.

SHARED RESPONSIBILITY MODEL

The Shared Responsibility model is a fundamental principle in cloud security, outlining the division of responsibilities between cloud service providers (CSPs) and their customers. While CSPs are accountable for securing the underlying cloud infrastructure, including hardware, software, and network components. Customers are responsible for safeguarding their data, applications, and configurations within the cloud. Misinterpretation of these roles can result in vulnerabilities and compliance breaches. This chapter will explore the specifics of the concept across various service types. Infrastructure-as-a-Service (IaaS), Platform-as-a-Service (PaaS), and Software-as-a-Service (SaaS) to help you comprehend your responsibilities and implement effective security protocols. Understanding and adhering to this model is important for mitigating risks and maximizing the benefits of secure cloud computing.

RESPONSIBILITIES

In cloud computing, it is necessary to comprehend the division of responsibilities between cloud providers and customers to maintain a secure and compliant environment. This division is governed by the shared responsibility model, a model that clearly outlines which security aspects are managed by the cloud provider and which are the customer's responsibility.

Cloud providers, such as AWS, Microsoft Azure, and Google Cloud, are responsible for securing the underlying infrastructure that powers the cloud. This includes physical security at data centres, maintaining hardware and network infrastructure, and managing system level software and patches. Cloud providers must also ensure service availability and compliance with applicable standards, such as ISO 27001 or SOC 2.

For example, in Infrastructure as a Service (IaaS), the provider manages components like virtual servers and storage infrastructure, but the customer must configure and secure the resources they deploy. Similarly, in Software as a Service (SaaS), the provider takes on more responsibility, covering the application layer, leaving customers to manage user access and data security.

Customers are accountable for securing the elements they control. This includes managing their data, configuring identity and access management (IAM), securing their applications, and ensuring proper use of security tools. In IaaS environments, this responsibility extends to operating system security, application patches, and virtual network configurations.

For example, if a customer misconfigures a storage bucket, leaving sensitive data exposed to the general internet public, the provider is not at fault. The customer is also responsible for implementing encryption, maintaining strong authentication policies, and adhering to compliance requirements relevant to their industry.

The division of responsibilities shifts based on the chosen model:

• IaaS: Customers manage the most, including the operating system, applications, and data security.

• PaaS: Providers handle the platform infrastructure, while customers focus on application security and access controls.

• SaaS: Providers manage almost everything except customer data and user access.

Misinterpreting the shared responsibility model can lead to vulnerabilities and data loss. For instance, assuming the provider handles everything may result in relaxed security practices on the customer's side. By clearly defining and adhering to their roles, both parties can collaborate effectively to ensure a secure and resilient cloud environment.

PROVIDER VS CUSTOMER RESPONSIBILITIES

In cloud computing, the shared responsibility model delineates the distribution of security and operational duties between cloud providers and customers, depending on the service model: Infrastructure as a Service (IaaS), Platform as a Service (PaaS), and Software as a Service (SaaS). Understanding these distinctions is crucial for effectively managing cloud environments and mitigating security risks.

In IaaS, cloud providers manage the foundational infrastructure, including physical hardware, networking, storage, and virtualization layers. Customers, however, are responsible for everything they build on top, such as operating systems, applications, and data.

For example, providers infrastructure hosting AWS EC2 or Azure Virtual Machines ensure the servers are running and patched, but customers must configure their operating system, firewalls, install updates, and secure their data. This model offers the most control to customers but requires significant technical expertise to manage securely.

In PaaS, providers take on more responsibilities, managing the underlying infrastructure, including operating systems, and middleware. This allows customers to focus solely on their applications and data.

For instance, the provider handles tasks like patching the operating system or maintaining the database server, while the customer ensures their application code is secure and access controls are properly configured. This model reduces operational complexity but still requires customers to prioritise application-level security.

In SaaS, providers manage nearly everything, including the application, infrastructure, and data hosting. Customers are primarily responsible for managing user access and securing the data they input.

For example, while Microsoft ensures the functionality and security of Office 365, it is up to the customer to configure multi-factor authentication (MFA), define user permissions, and secure sensitive documents.

Failure to understand these divisions can result in security gaps. For instance, assuming a provider secures user data in IaaS environments can lead to vulnerabilities and data loss or theft. By recognising their responsibilities, both providers and customers can work together to create strong, secure cloud environments tailored to an organisation's needs.

REAL WORLD SCENARIOS

Understanding the shared responsibility model in cloud security can be complex, and often lead to vulnerabilities in cloud environments. Real-world scenarios illustrate these misunderstandings and their consequences, emphasizing the importance of clearly defining roles between cloud providers and customers.

A retail company migrated its customer data to the cloud using an Infrastructure as a Service (IaaS) provider. Assuming the cloud provider managed all aspects of security, the company neglected to configure access permissions on its storage buckets. As a result, sensitive customer information, including credit card numbers, was exposed to the public internet.

While the cloud provider ensures the infrastructure hosting the storage buckets is secure, configuring access permissions is the customer's responsibility. Services like identity and access management (IAM) policies should be used to restrict access. This type of incident highlights the need for customers to actively secure data and manage permissions.

A start-up company built its web application on a Platform as a Service (PaaS) platform, assuming the provider would handle all security concerns. However, an attacker exploited a vulnerability in the application's code, leading to a data breach. The start-up blamed the provider for the breach, believing it was their responsibility to ensure security.

In PaaS, the provider secures the platform infrastructure, but the customer is responsible for the security of their applications and code. Regular vulnerability assessments and secure coding practices are necessary to mitigate such risks.

A healthcare organisation adopted a Software as a Service (SaaS) based electronic health records (EHR) solution. While the provider ensured the application and underlying infrastructure were secure, employees reused weak passwords across multiple accounts. This led to unauthorised access to sensitive patient data.

In SaaS, the provider secures the software and infrastructure, but customers must enforce strong user authentication practices, including multi-factor authentication (MFA) and password policies.

A financial firm assumed that its cloud provider's compliance certifications automatically covered their operations. However, during an audit, the firm was found non-compliant due to inadequate encryption of their data in transit.

While providers may meet compliance standards for their infrastructure, customers are responsible for ensuring their use of the cloud positions with industry regulations.

These scenarios underline the critical need for organisations to understand their responsibilities in respect of cloud security. Clear role definitions, regular training, and adopting best practices are vital to avoiding costly issues. By recognising and addressing these responsibilities, organisations can ensure a more secure and compliant cloud environment.

RESPONSIBILITY FAILURES

A mid-sized e-commerce firm moved its operations to a prominent Infrastructure as a Service (IaaS) cloud provider to enhance scalability and manage seasonal traffic fluctuations. Although the migration was successful, the company mistakenly assumed that the cloud provider was entirely responsible for data security. Consequently, they neglected to implement adequate access controls on their database.

Shortly after, a security expert discovered that the company's customer database was publicly accessible due to an incorrectly configured firewall rule. This database contained sensitive information, including names, email addresses, and payment details. The breach exposed the personal data of over 500,000 customers, leading to severe reputational damage and regulatory scrutiny under GDPR.

The failure stemmed from a misunderstanding of the shared responsibility model. While the cloud provider ensured the physical and virtual security of the infrastructure, it was the company's duty to configure security settings for the resources it deployed, including firewall rules, encryption, and user access permissions.

Following the breach, the company took several steps to rectify the issue and prevent future incidents:

1. Extensive security training: The IT team underwent training to better understand their responsibilities within the IaaS environment.

2. Implementation of best practices: The company adopted the principle of least privilege, ensuring that only authorised personnel could access critical resources.

3. Utilisation of cloud security services: They deployed a Cloud Security Posture Management (CSPM) solution to automate the detection of misconfigurations and provide real-time alerts.

4. Regular Audits: The organisation established regular security audits to identify and remediate vulnerabilities in their cloud environment.

5. Encryption: Data was encrypted both in transit and at rest to mitigate the impact of any potential future breaches.

These examples underscore the importance of understanding the division of responsibilities in cloud environments. Organisations cannot rely solely on cloud providers to secure their resources. Instead, they must proactively manage aspects under their control, such as access configurations, encryption, and compliance. By addressing these gaps, the e-commerce company was able to restore customer trust, enhance its security posture, and avoid further regulatory penalties. This resolution highlights the need for clear communication, training, and tools to effectively navigate shared responsibility in the cloud.

IDENTITY & ACCESS MANAGEMENT

Identity and Access Management (IAM) is the foundation of cloud security, permitting only authorised users and systems access to resources. By adhering to the principle of least privilege and using services such as role-based access control (RBAC) and multi-factor authentication (MFA), IAM serves as the primary access to your cloud environment. Inadequate identity management or overly permissive accounts can leave systems vulnerable to breaches and insider threats. This chapter delves into IAM's fundamental principles, best practices, and services across major cloud platforms, providing you with ways to strengthen access controls and mitigate risks in today's interconnected environments.

LEAST PRIVILEGE & RBAC

Identity and Access Management is a fundamental component of cloud security, ensuring that only authorised users and systems can access resources. Two important concepts within IAM are the principle of least privilege (PoLP) and role-based access control. Together, they form a strong foundation for minimizing security risks while maintaining operational efficiency.

The principle of least privilege specifies that users, applications, and systems should only possess the minimum permissions necessary to perform their tasks. This approach significantly reduces the attack surface and minimizes the risk of accidental or malicious misuse of resources. For instance, an employee responsible for generating reports should not have administrative access to the database. Excessive permissions can lead to unauthorised actions or make the system vulnerable if their credentials are compromised.

To implement PoLP effectively:

• Regularly review permissions, so that permissions align with current job responsibilities.

• Use time bound permissions, grant temporary permissions for tasks such as troubleshooting or project-based work.

• Monitor access logs, to detect any anomalies or violations in access logs.

RBAC assigns permissions to roles rather than individual users. Roles should be created based on job functions, and users are assigned to roles according to their responsibilities. For example, in a cloud environment, predefined roles like "Database

Administrator," "Developer," and "Read-Only Analyst"
can be defined with specific permissions.

RBAC simplifies permission management, particularly
in large organisations, by standardising access levels and
reducing the potential for errors. It also streamlines
onboarding and offboarding processes, as new users can
be quickly assigned to appropriate roles and leavers can
have permissions revoked.

To implement RBAC:

• Define roles clearly, so that roles position with
organisational workflows.

• Avoid overlapping roles, assigning multiple
overlapping roles to a single user, as it may lead to
excessive permissions.

• Periodically audit roles, adjust roles as organisational
needs develop.

When combined, PoLP and RBAC provide a powerful
way to for access control. PoLP ensures that permissions
within roles are limited to necessary actions, while RBAC
simplifies the management of those permissions at scale.

Implementing these principles not only strengthens security but also ensures compliance with regulatory requirements, such as GDPR for example. By minimizing access and closely managing permissions, organisations can effectively protect their cloud environments from unauthorised access and potential breaches.

MFA & PASSWORDLESS

In today's digital environment, strong authentication is necessary for safeguarding cloud environments and sensitive data from unauthorised access. Traditional passwords are often insufficient due to their vulnerability to brute-force attacks, credential theft, and user errors, and reusing weak passwords. Implementing advanced authentication methods like Multi-Factor Authentication (MFA) and passwordless solutions significantly enhances security and reduce these risks.

MFA necessitates users to provide two or more forms of verification to access a system. This typically involves combining something they know (a password), something they have (a security token), and something they are (biometric data). This has several benefits for the user:

• Enhanced security, if a password is compromised, additional verification layers, such as a one-time code or fingerprint scan, prevent unauthorised access.

• Wide adoption, MFA is available with most modern cloud platforms and services, making it a standard feature for securing accounts.

• Secure verification methods, time-based one-time passwords (TOTP) or hardware security keys for added security over SMS-based codes, which are vulnerable to SIM-swapping attacks.

• Account access control, use MFA for all privileged accounts and encourage its use for general users.

• User education, regularly educate users on recognising and reporting phishing attempts that aim to bypass MFA.

Passwordless authentication eliminates the need for traditional passwords, relying on more secure methods such as biometrics, hardware tokens, or cryptographic keys. Examples include FIDO2-compliant devices and single sign-on (SSO) platforms integrated with biometric authentication, and provide many benefits:

• Reduced attack surface, without passwords, there's no risk of credential theft or brute-force attacks.

• Improved user experience, users can authenticate consistently without remembering complex passwords.

• Enhanced compliance, many passwordless methods meet regulatory standards for strong authentication.

• Zero-trust integration, combining passwordless authentication with zero-trust principles, ensures users and devices are continuously verified.

For optimal security, organisations can combine these security methods. For instance, a passwordless login using a biometric scan can be paired with a second factor, such as a hardware key, to provide both convenience and strong security.

By adopting MFA and passwordless, organisations significantly enhance their defence against unauthorised access, phishing, and data breaches, creating a more secure and user-friendly authentication experience.

OVERPRIVILEGED USERS

In the domain of cloud security, misconfigurations and inadequate access controls create significant vulnerabilities. Two major issues organisations encounter are excessive user permissions and insufficient auditing. Both issues expose organisations to unnecessary security risks, potentially leading to data breaches, unauthorised access, and compliance failures. Understanding these issues is crucial for enhancing an organisation's cyber security posture.

Overprivileged users are individuals or systems granted more permissions than necessary to perform their job function. This issue is common, particularly in large organisations or environments where permissions are granted loosely or reactively.

When users or systems have excessive access, they can inadvertently or maliciously access sensitive data, modify configurations, or escalate their privileges. For instance, a marketing employee might have unnecessary access to financial data or production systems, creating opportunities for either accidental data leakage or malicious activity. The general security risks to remember are:

• Increased attack surface, compromising an overprivileged account can grant attackers access to a wide range of sensitive data and interconnected systems.

• Privilege escalation, overprivileged accounts can be exploited by attackers to escalate their privileges, leading to more wider impacting breaches.

• Regulatory and compliance risks, many regulatory frameworks, such as GDPR or PCI-DSS, require strict control over user access. Overprivileged accounts can violate these regulations, leading to fines and legal issues. To mitigate these risks, organisations should generally:

• Apply the principle of least privilege, users should only have the minimum access necessary for their role.

• Use role-based access control, permissions are assigned based on predefined roles rather than granting permissions to individual users.

• Regularly review permissions, audit user access to ensure that permissions remain appropriate as roles change.

Auditing is necessary for maintaining and ensuring that security controls are functioning as intended. A lack of regular security audits and reviews leaves organisations vulnerable to security breaches and configuration errors.

Without audits, organisations may fail to detect misconfigurations, unauthorised changes, or access violations. For example, an administrator might inadvertently leave an open access point or fail to implement necessary security patches, leading to vulnerabilities that can be exploited over time.

• Undetected security incidents, unauthorised access or malicious actions may go unnoticed for extended periods, leading to greater damage.

• Compliance violations, many industries require regular security audits to ensure data protection and regulatory compliance, leading to penalties for missing compliance.

• Missed opportunities for improvement, regular audits provide insights into potential weaknesses, allowing organisations to address vulnerabilities before they are exploited.

To address these issues effectively, particularly in large organisations that tend to be more affected with compounded issues over time:

• Automate auditing processes, use tools that automate the collection and analysis of logs to ensure timely detection of anomalies.

• Conduct regular access audits, review user roles, permissions, and activities to ensure they are in line with the principle of least privilege.

• Implement continuous monitoring, use tools that offer real-time monitoring to detect suspicious activities promptly.

Ensuring that users are granted appropriate levels of access and implementing consistent audit practices, organisations can reduce the risk of data breaches, improve regulatory compliance, and maintain a strong security posture. Regular reviews, automated tools, and strong access controls are necessary to mitigating these common but preventable security issues.

AWS IAM, AZURE ENTRA, GOOGLE IAM

Identity and Access Management is an important component of cloud security, enabling organisations to control who has access to their cloud resources and what actions they are allowed to perform. Cloud service providers AWS, Microsoft Azure, and Google Cloud offer extensive IAM services tailored to their platforms. These are AWS IAM, Azure Active Entra (formerly Azure AD), and Google Cloud IAM. Each service helps users adhere to core IAM principles such as least privilege and role-based access control.

AWS IAM is a versatile tool for managing access to AWS resources. It allows organisations to create and manage users, groups, and roles, assigning fine-grained permissions through policies. Features include:

• Policies, JSON-based documents that define permissions for resources.

• Roles, temporary credentials for applications or services requiring specific access.

• Access keys and MFA, enhance security for programmatic access and interactive sessions.

• Service Control Policies (SCPs), for governance at the organisational level.

For example, a development team can use AWS IAM roles to grant temporary access to deploy applications without exposing permanent credentials.

Azure Entra extends IAM capabilities with a focus on identity management for enterprise users. It integrates with Microsoft 365 and hybrid cloud environments, making it popular for organisations using Azure and Microsoft services.

• Conditional access allows dynamic policies based on user behaviour, device status, or location.

• Integration with on-premises directories, facilitates hybrid environments.

• Azure role-based access control manages permissions for Azure resources.

• Identity protection uses machine learning to detect and mitigate identity risks.

For example, a healthcare organisation can use Azure Entra to enforce multi-factor authentication and conditional access for compliance with health regulations.

Google Cloud IAM provides centralised control over permissions for Google Cloud resources. Its simplicity and integration with Google Workspace make it suitable for diverse business needs.

• Predefined roles, simplifies permissions by bundling common access requirements.

• Custom roles, offers granular control for specific use cases.

• IAM policies, assign permissions at the resource, project, or organisation level.

• Workload identity federation allows secure identity authentication without exposing credentials.

For example, a media company can use Google Cloud IAM to assign predefined roles to developers, ensuring they only access resources necessary for their tasks.

The choice between AWS IAM, Azure Entra, and Google Cloud IAM depends on the organisation's cloud platform and business needs. Each service provides strong features for managing access, ensuring strong security, and achieving compliance in cloud environments. By leveraging these IAM services effectively, organisations can minimize risks and maintain control over their cloud resources.

DATA PROTECTION

Protecting data in the cloud is necessary for maintaining trust, upholding privacy, and adhering to regulatory standards. Cloud environments pose unique challenges, including safeguarding data at rest, in transit, and during processing, while at the same time addressing data residency and sovereignty concerns. Encryption is a crucial component, securing sensitive information against unauthorised access. Compliance with frameworks such as GDPR, HIPAA, and PCI-DSS adds another layer of complexity. This chapter delves into the tools, techniques, and strategies for strong cloud data protection, enabling you to achieve a balance between innovation and security in an ever-evolving regulatory and threat environment.

ENCRYPTION

Encryption is a fundamental security measure that safeguards data by converting it into unreadable formats using cryptographic algorithms. This ensures that even if data is intercepted or accessed without authorisation, it cannot be understood without the appropriate decryption key. Effective encryption strategies cover three states of data, at rest, in transit, and during processing.

Encryption at rest protects data stored on physical or virtual devices, such as hard drives, cloud storage, or databases. This ensures that even if the storage medium is compromised through theft or unauthorised access, the data remains secure.

• Full disk encryption encrypts entire storage drives.

• Database encryption secures specific tables or fields.

• File-level encryption protects individual files.

For example, encrypting sensitive customer information stored in cloud databases or financial records on an internal server prevents unauthorised access during breaches.

Encryption in transit secures data while it travels between systems, such as from a user's device to a cloud server or between microservices within an application. This is important for protecting data against interception attacks, such as man-in-the-middle (MITM) attacks.

• Transport Layer Security (TLS) secures HTTP connections (commonly shown in the browser as HTTPS and a padlock).

• Virtual Private Networks (VPN), encrypt all traffic between endpoints.

• Secure File Transfer Protocols (SFTP), ensure encrypted data exchanges.

For example, when users log into a SaaS platform, TLS ensures that their credentials and session data are encrypted as they travel across the internet.

Encryption during processing ensures that data remains secure even while it is being used or analysed. This is the most challenging state to secure since data typically needs to be decrypted for processing. Technologies like homomorphic encryption and confidential computing address this as required.

• Homomorphic encryption allows computations on encrypted data without decryption.

• Confidential computing uses hardware-based enclaves to process encrypted data securely.

For example, a financial institution using homomorphic encryption can analyse encrypted customer transactions without exposing sensitive information, even to internal systems.

By implementing encryption for data at rest, in transit, and during processing, organisations can ensure extensive protection across all stages of the data lifecycle. This layered approach minimizes risks and helps meet compliance requirements for data privacy and security. Strong algorithms like AES-256, combined with techniques such as homomorphic encryption and secure access controls, provide strong protection against unauthorised access and breaches.

DATA RESIDENCY & SOVEREIGNTY

Data Residency are the geographical location where data is stored. Organisations often select specific locations to comply with regional regulations or ensure proximity to their operations.

Data Sovereignty pertains to the legal control over data based on the laws of the country where the data resides. Even if data is stored abroad, it may still be subject to the laws of its origin country. For instance, data stored in an EU country is governed by GDPR, which imposes strict privacy and security requirements. Similarly, data in the United States may be subject to the CLOUD Act, enabling U.S. authorities to access data stored by U.S.-based companies, even if stored overseas.

Data residency and sovereignty issues can complicate compliance, particularly when organisations fail to account for the legal requirements of different jurisdictions. Including:

1. Regulatory Compliance

Regulations like GDPR, HIPAA, and Australia's Privacy Act mandate specific controls over where and how data is stored. Non-compliance can result in large fines and reputational damage.

2. Cross-Border Data Transfers

Moving data across borders often requires compliance with specific frameworks, such as Standard Contractual Clauses (SCCs) under GDPR. Organisations must ensure lawful transfer mechanisms or face legal challenges.

3. Operational Complexity

Managing data across multiple jurisdictions with differing legal requirements adds complexity to operations, necessitating strong governance strategies.

4. Risk of Government Access

Data sovereignty laws can grant local governments access to data stored within their jurisdiction, raising concerns about data privacy and security. This is particularly relevant in regions with weaker privacy protections.

There are some common actions that should be performed as soon as possible, particularly for new and emerging companies. Larger more mature companies will have the additional challenge of legacy data and services to deal with:

• Understanding local laws, conduct thorough legal reviews for all jurisdictions where data is stored or processed.

• Leverage cloud service providers, many cloud providers, such as AWS, Azure, and Google Cloud, offer services to help define data residency and enforce compliance.

• Implement data segmentation, use region-specific storage to ensure data remains in compliance with local regulations.

• Use encryption, secure data both in transit and at rest to minimize risks associated with unauthorised government access.

Navigating data residency and sovereignty issues is necessary for compliance in today's global cloud environment. By understanding regional regulations and implementing strategies aligned to them, organisations can mitigate risks and ensure their cloud operations remain secure and compliant.

KEY MANAGEMENT

Key management is the foundation of data encryption and security in cloud environments, ensuring that cryptographic keys used for encryption, decryption, and authentication are securely generated, stored, and managed. Proper key management minimizes the risk of unauthorised access, ensuring compliance with industry standards and regulatory requirements. Two important approaches to key management are hardware security modules (HSMs) and cloud-native key management tools.

HSMs are physical or virtual devices specifically designed to generate, manage, and store cryptographic keys securely. They provide high levels of security, performance, and compliance for encryption needs.

Tamper-Resistant, HSMs are built with tamper-evident and tamper-proof mechanisms to prevent unauthorised access. They use hardware-based security, dedicated hardware ensures cryptographic operations are isolated from other systems, reducing attack surfaces. HSMs often meet stringent regulatory standards, such as FIPS 140-2 Level 3 or higher. Example uses include:

• Protecting sensitive financial data for payment processing.

• Securing root keys for certificate authorities (CAs).

• Managing encryption keys for critical systems in on-premises or hybrid environments.

For example, AWS Cloud HSM and Azure Dedicated HSM provide cloud accessible HSM solutions for scalability while retaining hardware-level security.

Cloud-native key management tools, such as AWS Key Management Service (KMS), Azure Key Vault, and Google Cloud Key Management, simplify encryption key lifecycle management within the cloud provider's ecosystem. Cloud native services provide consistent integration with other cloud services for automated encryption at rest and in transit. Provides global scalability and redundancy for key storage and usage. Utilises IAM policies and roles to restrict access to encryption keys. Includes built-in logging enabling organisations to monitor key usage for compliance and security anomalies. Example use cases include:

• Encrypting cloud storage buckets, databases, and message queues.

• Managing keys for serverless functions and microservices.

• Enabling customer-managed encryption keys (CMEKs) for greater control over data security.

While HSMs offer superior security for highly sensitive environments, they can be very costly and complex to manage. Cloud-native tools provide more affordable, greater flexibility, scalability, and ease of use, making them ideal for many cloud-centric organisations. In some situations, a hybrid approach, where HSMs generate and store root keys while cloud-native tools manage operational keys, though this is not common.

Effective key management is important for maintaining strong encryption and ensuring data security. Organisations must evaluate their specific needs, balancing business needs, security, scalability, and cost, to choose between HSMs, cloud-native tools, or a combination of both.

COMPLIANCE CHALLENGES

Compliance with data protection and privacy regulations is a fundamental requirement for organisations handling sensitive data. Regulations such as the General Data Protection Regulation, Health Insurance Portability and Accountability Act, and Payment Card Industry Data Security Standard impose strict controls over how personal and sensitive data is collected, processed, stored, and transmitted. However, navigating these compliance frameworks presents various challenges, particularly in cloud environments where data is dispersed across multiple jurisdictions.

GDPR is a European Union regulation that governs the handling of personal data of EU residents. It applies to any organisation, regardless of location, that processes or stores the personal data of EU individuals. There are a few areas to consider:

• GDPR grants individuals rights such as data access, rectification, and the "right to be forgotten." Ensuring that these rights are respected and implemented can be challenging, particularly when data is stored across multiple cloud platforms.

• GDPR requires that data transferred outside the EU must meet specific criteria to ensure that the receiving country provides adequate data protection. This can be complicated when data flows across borders, especially with changing international data transfer agreements.

• GDPR mandates that data breaches must be reported within 72 hours. Organisations must have the necessary processes and tools in place to detect, investigate, and report breaches promptly.

HIPAA is a U.S. regulation that sets standards for the protection of health information, specifically for healthcare providers, insurers, and their partners. HIPAA ensures the confidentiality, integrity, and availability of Protected Health Information. There are a few areas to consider:

• HIPAA requires encryption of PHI both at rest and in transit. Ensuring that all PHI is encrypted and that encryption keys are properly managed.

• HIPAA mandates strict access control policies, ensuring that only authorised individuals can access PHI.

• HIPAA requires healthcare organisations to sign BAAs with third-party vendors who handle PHI. Ensuring that cloud vendors comply with HIPAA and establishing clear contractual agreements.

PCI-DSS is a set of security standards designed to protect cardholder data in payment systems. It applies to all entities that store, process, or transmit payment card information.

What compliance challenges exist?

• PCI-DSS requires that sensitive cardholder data be encrypted and that access to it be strictly controlled. Managing this in a cloud environment where resources may scale dynamically adds complexity to ensure all sensitive data is protected.

- PCI-DSS mandates the continuous monitoring of systems and the logging of all access to cardholder data.

- PCI-DSS compliance also extends to third-party providers, including cloud services. Ensuring that these vendors meet PCI-DSS requirements requires careful evaluation and ongoing monitoring.

The challenges of complying with GDPR, HIPAA, and PCI-DSS in cloud environments are significant but manageable with the right services, people, and processes. Organisations must continuously monitor their data protection practices, integrate strong encryption, and access controls, as well as maintain strong vendor relationships to ensure compliance. As cloud environments become more complex, leveraging cloud-native compliance tools and automating processes can help ease the burden of compliance.

THREAT AND INCIDENT RESPONSE

Cloud environments present distinct challenges for threat detection and response, necessitating a departure from the more traditional security. The nature of cloud workloads, coupled with the shared responsibility model, demands continuous monitoring and rapid response. Tools such as Security Information and Event Management (SIEM) systems and cloud-native solutions offer critical visibility into potential threats. Effective incident response frameworks, including those from NIST and SANS, ensure organisations are prepared to handle breaches. This chapter explores the frameworks, tools, and real-world practices for threat detection and incident response, helping organisations mitigate damage and recover efficiently in the face of evolving cloud threats.

CYBER THREATS

In the domain of cloud security, organisations face a varied array of cybersecurity threats that can compromise data integrity, confidentiality, and availability. It is crucial to understand these threats and their potential consequences to safeguard cloud-based systems and data effectively.

Malware refers to any type of malicious software designed to gain unauthorised access, damage, or disrupt systems. This includes viruses, worms, ransomware, spyware, and trojans. Malware can be delivered through phishing emails, compromised websites, or infected software downloads to name a few. The impact can vary and be severe:

• Malware can alter, delete, or steal data, leading to loss of critical information.

• Ransomware, are a specific type of malware that encrypts data and demands payment for its release, paralysing an organisations' operations.

• Malware can create backdoors into networks, allowing attackers to gain continuous access for espionage or further attacks.

Some mitigations include implementing endpoint security solutions to detect malware. Regularly updating software to patch vulnerabilities reduces the risk of infection. Use of network segmentation and strong firewalls minimizes the blast impact to other devices if an infection occurs.

Phishing is a type of social engineering attack where attackers impersonate legitimate entities, such as banks or cloud providers, to trick individuals into divulging sensitive information (usernames, passwords, and financial details). This can occur via email, social media, or text messages, effectively through any communication methos to a human.

• Attackers can use stolen credentials to gain unauthorised access to cloud systems and sensitive data.

• Phishing scams can trick employees into transferring money or giving attackers access to banking systems.

• Organisations suffer loss of customer trust when they are the victims of a phishing attack.

Mitigations include, installing anti-phishing tools and email filtering systems. It is important to conduct regular employee training on recognising phishing attempts. Use multi-factor authentication to protect accounts from credential theft as this is a common issue now where password collections are shared openly on the Internet.

DDoS attacks overwhelm a system, server, or network with a massive volume of traffic, making it unavailable to legitimate users. These attacks can be used to disrupt business operations or serve as a diversion for other malicious activities. Cloud services, websites, or applications can become inaccessible, leading to operational disruptions. The attack consumes server and network resources, potentially increasing cloud infrastructure costs. Repeated service interruptions can harm an organisation's reputation and erode customer confidence.

Mitigations include deploying DDoS protection services from cloud providers like AWS Shield, Azure DDoS Protection, or Cloudflare. Implement rate limiting and traffic filtering techniques. Also, use content delivery networks (CDNs) to absorb and mitigate traffic spikes.

Insider threats occur when individuals within an organisation, such as employees, contractors, or business partners, misuse their access to compromise data or systems. These threats are particularly dangerous because insiders typically have authorised access, making it more difficult to detect malicious actions.

Insiders can steal sensitive data for financial gain or to harm the organisation. Malicious insiders can alter or destroy critical systems, causing significant damage. Insider actions may lead to breaches of regulatory compliance, resulting in legal repercussions.

Mitigations include building strict access controls based on the principle of least privilege. Monitor user behaviour with advanced analytics and anomaly detection tools. Conduct regular audits of user activities and access logs.

Malware, phishing, DDoS attacks, and insider threats are significant security concerns for organisations operating within the cloud. While each threat comes with unique challenges. Unique mitigations are required, such as multi-layered defences, user education, and real-time monitoring, which can help reduce their impact and protect valuable data and systems. Regular threat assessments and a proactive approach to security are necessary for maintaining a resilient cloud security posture.

THREAT DETECTION

In the ever-changing environment of cybersecurity, effective threat detection is most important in safeguarding cloud infrastructure. As cyber threats escalate in volume and complexity, organisations require more sophisticated tools to monitor, analyse, and respond to potential security incidents in real-time. Two prominent categories of threat detection tools are Security Information and Event Management (SIEM) solutions and cloud-native logging solutions. Both play important roles in securing cloud environments; both have unique features and benefits.

SIEM systems are designed to provide extensive security monitoring by collecting, aggregating, and analysing log data from various sources within an IT environment.

These tools offer real-time analysis of security alerts generated by applications, network devices, and other IT infrastructure. SIEM systems are necessary for identifying suspicious activity, detecting threats, and ensuring compliance with regulatory requirements.

SIEM aggregates logs from different systems, networks, and endpoints into a centralised platform for analysis. SIEM provides real-time analysis and alerting, helping security teams detect threats as they occur. They use correlation rules and machine learning to identify patterns of behaviour that may indicate a security breach.

SIEM tools often integrate with incident response systems, this can provide automated or manual actions to contain or mitigate threats.

Cloud-native logging solutions are designed to provide visibility and monitoring capabilities for organisations leveraging cloud platforms. Unlike traditional SIEM tools, cloud-native logging solutions are purpose-built for cloud environments, offering consistent integration with cloud services, scalability, and flexibility. These solutions collect and analyse log data generated by cloud resources, applications, and user activities.

Cloud-native solutions are tightly integrated with cloud platforms like AWS, Azure, and Google Cloud, making it easier to collect and analyse logs from cloud-based services. Cloud-native logging tools scale automatically to handle large volumes of log data without the need for manual intervention or infrastructure management.

These solutions provide powerful search and query features that enable security teams to efficiently analyse logs and identify security incidents. Cloud-native logging solutions often include machine learning and behavioural analytics to detect anomalous activities, improving the speed and accuracy of threat detection.

While both SIEM systems and cloud-native logging solutions provide critical capabilities for threat detection, their use cases differ. SIEM tools are typically better suited for enterprises with complex, hybrid IT environments where data from on-premises infrastructure needs to be analysed alongside cloud-based resources. They are also valuable for organisations that require detailed reporting and compliance management.

Cloud-native logging solutions, on the other hand, are ideal for organisations that predominantly operate in the cloud. These tools offer native integration with cloud services, providing real-time visibility into cloud resources and applications without the overhead of managing on-premises infrastructure.

Both SIEM systems and cloud-native logging solutions are important components of an organisation's security toolset. By combining the advanced analytics and threat correlation of SIEM with the scalability and integration of cloud-native logging solutions, organisations can improve their threat detection capabilities, respond to incidents faster, and ensure extensive security monitoring across both on-premises and cloud environments.

INCIDENT RESPONSE FRAMEWORKS

Incident response is an important aspect of any organisation's cybersecurity capability, focusing on identifying, managing, and mitigating security incidents. Two widely adopted frameworks in the industry are the National Institute of Standards and Technology (NIST) framework and the SANS Institute framework.

The NIST framework, detailed in special publication 800-61, provides a formal, structured approach to handling cybersecurity incidents. It emphasizes the importance of preparing for incidents, detecting them, and responding effectively.

1. Preparation phase focuses on establishing the foundation for an effective incident response capability. It includes developing an incident response policy, creating an incident response team, setting up tools and technologies, and ensuring that personnel are trained and aware of their roles in the event of an incident.

2. Detection and analysis phase involves identifying the incident, analysing its scope, and understanding its impact. It emphasizes the importance of accurate detection tools, monitoring, and logs for incident identification.

3. Containment, Eradication, and Recovery phases, the priority is to contain the incident to prevent further damage. Following containment, the root cause is eradicated, and recovery processes are initiated to restore affected systems and services to normal operations.

4. Post-Incident Activity phase, the incident is resolved, post-incident analysis is conducted to understand what happened, why it happened, and how future incidents can be prevented. This phase includes reporting, documentation, and refining response processes.

NIST is a widely recognized and extensive framework. It focuses on continuous improvement through post-incident analysis. Emphasizes the importance of preparation and readiness.

The SANS Institute provides a simplified yet highly effective incident response methodology, often referred to as the SANS Incident Response Lifecycle. The SANS framework is based on a six-phase model that closely mirrors the NIST framework but with slightly different terminology and emphasis on specific actions.

1. Preparation phase focuses on ensuring the organisation has the necessary tools, policies, and personnel in place to handle incidents. It involves training staff, deploying incident response tools, and establishing incident-handling procedures.

2. Identification phase involves detecting potential incidents and determining their scope. It requires effective monitoring systems and the analysis of logs and alerts.

3. Containment phase, once an incident is identified, containment is important to prevent further spread or damage. This phase includes steps like isolating compromised systems or restricting access to affected resources.

4. Eradication phase, after containment, the root cause of the incident must be removed, and vulnerabilities should be addressed to prevent recurrence.

5. Recovery phase, systems are restored to normal operations, and affected systems are closely monitored to ensure that they are free from threats.

6. Lessons learned phase, focuses on reviewing the incident response process, updating response plans, and applying insights gained to improve future incident handling.

SANS is simple and easy to understand, making it accessible for organisations of all sizes. Focuses on actionable steps that can be implemented quickly. Emphasizes the importance of documentation and learning from each incident.

While both NIST and SANS have similar overall goals, they differ in their approach to incident response. NIST's framework is more detailed, structured, and suited for larger organisations with complex IT infrastructures, especially those with compliance and regulatory requirements. SANS offers a more straightforward, practical approach that can be easily adopted by organisations with fewer resources or those that need a quicker, actionable plan.

Both the NIST and SANS frameworks provide necessary guidelines for managing and mitigating cybersecurity incidents. Organisations should evaluate their specific needs, resources, and complexity to determine which framework is best suited to their environment. Regardless of the chosen framework, an effective incident response plan is critical for minimizing the impact of security incidents, maintaining operational continuity, and improving overall security posture.

EXAMPLE CASE

The effectiveness of an incident response can significantly influence an organisation's security posture, reputation, and financial stability.

Target Company Data Breach: A Case Study in Cloud Security Failures

In the 2013 holiday season, Target, a prominent U.S. retailer, suffered a substantial data breach. The incident was started by hackers exploiting compromised credentials from a third-party vendor. This breach compromised over 40 million credit and debit card accounts and exposed personal data from an additional 70 million customers.

Target's security team failed to identify the intrusion for several weeks after the breach occurred. During this period, the attackers remained undetected, stealing sensitive data, and installing malware on point-of-sale terminals. Target's security systems flagged suspicious activity, but these alerts were either ignored or not thoroughly investigated in a timely manner. This delay allowed the attackers to move laterally across the network.

The breach originated from compromised credentials of a third-party vendor. Target did not adequately secure vendor access to its systems, providing hackers with a pathway into its network. Once the breach was detected, Target faced challenges in containment. Although the company eventually implemented measures to halt data exfiltration, the attack had already caused significant damage.

The breach incurred over $200 million in direct expenses and led to the resignation of several top executives, including the Chief Information Officer and Chief Information Security Officer. The incident also severely damaged Target's brand reputation and eroded customer trust.

Target's failed response highlights how delays in detecting and addressing threats, along with poor vendor management, can lead to severe financial and reputational damage. This example underscores the necessity for organisations to develop and regularly test incident response plans to ensure they are prepared to handle cybersecurity incidents effectively.

EXAMPLE CASE

The effectiveness of an incident response can significantly influence an organisation's security posture, reputation, and financial stability.

Target Company Data Breach: A Case Study in Cloud Security Failures

In the 2013 holiday season, Target, a prominent U.S. retailer, suffered a substantial data breach. The incident was started by hackers exploiting compromised credentials from a third-party vendor. This breach compromised over 40 million credit and debit card accounts and exposed personal data from an additional 70 million customers.

Target's security team failed to identify the intrusion for several weeks after the breach occurred. During this period, the attackers remained undetected, stealing sensitive data, and installing malware on point-of-sale terminals. Target's security systems flagged suspicious activity, but these alerts were either ignored or not thoroughly investigated in a timely manner. This delay allowed the attackers to move laterally across the network.

The breach originated from compromised credentials of a third-party vendor. Target did not adequately secure vendor access to its systems, providing hackers with a pathway into its network. Once the breach was detected, Target faced challenges in containment. Although the company eventually implemented measures to halt data exfiltration, the attack had already caused significant damage.

The breach incurred over $200 million in direct expenses and led to the resignation of several top executives, including the Chief Information Officer and Chief Information Security Officer. The incident also severely damaged Target's brand reputation and eroded customer trust.

Target's failed response highlights how delays in detecting and addressing threats, along with poor vendor management, can lead to severe financial and reputational damage. This example underscores the necessity for organisations to develop and regularly test incident response plans to ensure they are prepared to handle cybersecurity incidents effectively.

SECURING CLOUD INFRASTRUCTURE

Ensuring the security of your cloud infrastructure is most important to safeguarding the core of your cloud environment. Virtual networks, including Virtual Private Clouds (VPCs) and subnets, serve as the backbone of secure communication. Compute resources such as virtual machines, containers, and serverless functions are the engines that power cloud operations. However, misconfigurations, unauthorised access, and emerging threats can expose these elements to substantial risks. This chapter delves into the principles of cloud infrastructure security, focusing on services like security groups, firewalls, and workload protection. By implementing these measures, organisations can fortify their virtual networks and compute resources, creating a resilient and secure cloud ecosystem.

VPC, SUBNETS & SECURITY GROUPS

Cloud networking is the foundation of modern cloud infrastructure, enabling organisations to create secure and scalable environments for their applications and services. At the heart of cloud networking are three fundamental components, virtual private clouds, subnets, and security groups. These elements collectively provide isolation, segmentation, and strong security for resources hosted in the cloud. It is also important to point out that while the terminology may vary depending on the cloud service provider used, the function and purpose is the same.

A VPC is a logically isolated section of a cloud provider's infrastructure. It allows organisations to create their own virtual networks within the shared resources of the cloud while maintaining privacy and control.

A VPC ensures that resources within it are isolated from other customers' resources, providing a secure environment for applications and data. Users can define IP address ranges, subnets, and routing tables, tailoring the network to their specific needs. VPCs can connect to on-premises data centres through VPNs or dedicated connections, enabling hybrid cloud architectures. VPCs serve as the foundation for deploying cloud resources, such as virtual machines, databases, and containers, with configurable network access controls.

Subnets are subdivisions within a VPC that further segment the network into smaller, more manageable units. Subnets can be defined as public or private based on their accessibility from the internet.

1. Public Subnets, are connected to the internet and used for resources that require public access, such as web servers.

2. Private Subnets are not directly accessible from the internet and are typically used for backend resources like databases or application servers.

3. Subnets allow efficient allocation of IP address ranges within a VPC.

By segmenting resources, subnets help improve performance, simplify management, and enhance security by isolating sensitive workloads.

Security groups act as virtual firewalls for cloud resources, controlling inbound and outbound traffic at the instance level. Security groups use rules to define allowed traffic based on protocols, ports, and source/destination IPs. Once a connection is allowed, return traffic is automatically permitted, simplifying configurations. Security groups are associated with individual resources, offering granular control. Security groups are necessary for enforcing the principle of least privilege, ensuring that only necessary traffic is allowed to and from resources.

In a typical cloud networking setup, a VPC provides the overarching network. Within the VPC, subnets divide resources into logical zones, such as public and private segments. Security groups then provide fine-grained access control for individual resources within these subnets.

VPCs, subnets, and security groups form the core building blocks of cloud networking. Together, they enable organisations to design secure, scalable, and highly customizable network environments in the cloud. By understanding and effectively configuring these components, businesses can ensure strong connectivity, efficient resource management, and strong security for their cloud deployments.

VIRTUAL MACHINES, CONTAINERS & SERVERLESS

Ensuring the integrity of applications and data in cloud environments is critical. Workloads in these environments are typically hosted on virtual machines, containers, or serverless functions, each necessitating unique security measures tailored to their architecture and use cases.

VMs emulate physical servers and are widely used for running traditional workloads. They provide strong isolation between instances, as each VM runs its own operating system (OS) on virtualized hardware. Each VM requires management to:

1. Regularly update the OS and software to mitigate vulnerabilities. However, automated patching tools can streamline this process.
2. Implement strict access controls using Identity and Access Management roles, SSH key pairs, and multi-factor authentication.
3. Use firewalls, security groups, and Virtual Private Clouds to limit exposure to public networks.
4. Deploy antivirus and intrusion detection/prevention systems (IDS/IPS) on VM instances.

VMs offer strong compatibility for legacy applications, but their security relies heavily on proper configuration and regular monitoring.

Containers package applications and their dependencies into lightweight, portable units that run on a shared host OS. Tools like Docker and Kubernetes are commonly used for container orchestration and deployment. Containers require a different type of management:

1. Require trusted base images and scan them for vulnerabilities using tools like Trivy or Clair.
2. Enforce resource and process isolation using container runtime security features and namespaces.
3. Limit permissions for containers using Role-Based Access Control in orchestration platforms like Kubernetes.
4. Define network policies to restrict communication between containers and external services.
5. Monitor container behaviour for anomalies using tools like Falco or Aqua Security.

Containers improve scalability and efficiency but introduce risks like privilege escalation if not correctly secured and configured.

Serverless functions, such as AWS Lambda, Azure Functions, or Google Cloud Functions, run code in response to events without managing any infrastructure. This service abstracts infrastructure responsibilities, reducing the attack surface but introducing new security considerations. Security management include:

1. Use of least privilege principles when assigning IAM roles to functions.
2. Securely handle input to prevent injection attacks and other vulnerabilities.
3. Regularly update and scan libraries and dependencies for known vulnerabilities.
4. Secure the triggers (e.g., API Gateway, storage buckets) that invoke serverless functions.

Serverless workloads benefit from the cloud provider's managed security features but require monitoring in securing the application layer.

Protecting workloads in cloud environments requires tailored security practices based on the underlying technology. VMs demand extensive OS and network security, containers require strong image and runtime security, and serverless functions call for precise access control and dependency management. By adopting best practices and leveraging cloud-native security tools, organisations can safeguard their workloads and mitigate risks in diverse cloud architectures.

FIREWALLS AND IDS

In cloud environments, network security is an important concern against cyber threats. Two fundamental tools for securing network traffic are firewalls and intrusion detection systems (IDS). These tools play distinct yet complementary roles in safeguarding data and applications from unauthorised access and malicious activity.

Firewalls are the primary line of defence in network security. They monitor and control incoming and outgoing traffic based on predetermined security rules. Firewalls can be hardware-based, software-based, or cloud-native, and their primary goal is to enforce access control by filtering traffic.

1. Network Firewalls, operate at the network perimeter, analysing traffic at the protocol and port level to block unauthorised access.

2. Application Firewalls, focus on securing specific applications by inspecting data packets and identifying threats at the application layer.

3. Cloud Firewalls, are designed for cloud environments, such as AWS WAF, Azure Firewall, or Google Cloud Firewall. They are scalable and provide Centralised management for distributed architectures.

Firewalls help to enforce the principle of least privilege by restricting access to critical resources. They block known malicious IPs, unauthorised protocols, and traffic patterns that indicate attacks. Security administrators can define rules tailored to specific workloads or compliance requirements.

IDS tools detect and alert administrators about potential security breaches by monitoring network traffic and analysing it for suspicious activity. Unlike firewalls, which prevent unauthorised access, IDS focuses on identifying threats that have bypassed perimeter defences.

1. Network-Based IDS (NIDS), monitor traffic across the entire network to detect anomalies and potential threats.

2. Host-Based IDS (HIDS), operate on individual hosts, analysing logs, system files, and other data for malicious activity.

• Threat Detection IDS tools identify threats like malware, DDoS attacks, or unauthorised data exfiltration.

• Behavioural Analysis Advanced IDS solutions use machine learning to detect unknown threats by analysing deviations from normal behaviour.

• Alerting and Reporting, IDS systems generate alerts for suspicious activities, helping administrators respond quickly.

Firewalls are proactive, focusing on preventing threats by controlling access, while IDS tools are reactive, identifying threats that have already penetrated defences. When used together, they provide a layered defence approach to network security.

Firewalls and IDS tools are necessary components of a strong network security programme. Firewalls establish a strong perimeter defence by filtering traffic, while IDS tools enhance visibility into potential threats. By integrating these tools and leveraging cloud-native solutions, organisations can effectively secure their networks against evolving cyber threats.

COMMON MISCONFIGURATIONS

Misconfigurations in cloud environments are a primary cause of data breaches, compliance violations, and operational disruptions. These issues often stem from the complexity of cloud services, inadequate training, or oversight during deployment. Understanding and addressing common misconfigurations is necessary for maintaining a secure cloud environment.

Challenge: Misconfigured storage buckets, such as AWS S3, Azure Blob, or Google Cloud Storage, frequently allow public access, exposing sensitive data.

Solution: To minimise these risks, disable public access unless explicitly required. Use Identity and Access Management Grant least privilege access using IAM policies. Utilise cloud-native tools like AWS Config, Azure Security Centre, or Google Cloud Policy Analyzer to audit storage bucket permissions.

Challenge: Granting overprivileged access to users, applications, or services can lead to privilege escalation and unauthorised activities.

Solution: To minimise these risks, ensure entities only have permissions necessary for their tasks. Group users by job function using RBAC. Use tools like AWS IAM Access Analyzer, Azure Privileged Identity Management, or GCP IAM Recommendations to audit permissions.

Challenge: Overly permissive security group rules, such as open inbound traffic on sensitive ports (e.g., SSH or RDP), increase the attack surface.

Solution: To minimise these risks, limit access to necessary IP ranges and use VPNs for remote access. Only allow necessary ports to be open. Regularly review security group configurations and set up automated alerts for rule changes.

Challenge: Using single-factor authentication, weak passwords, or failing to enforce MFA exposes accounts to brute force attacks and credential theft.

Solution: To minimise these risks, require MFA for all accounts, especially for privileged users. Enforce complexity and expiration rules for passwords. Consider using passwordless methods like FIDO2 or OAuth-based solutions.

Challenge: Failing to apply security patches to operating systems, applications, or container images can leave known vulnerabilities unaddressed.

Solution: To minimise these risks, enable automatic patching for cloud-managed services and virtual machines. Regularly update container images and use tools like Trivy or Clair for vulnerability scanning. Deploy a patch management solution that tracks and enforces updates across your environment.

Challenge: Inadequate or missing logging reduces visibility of security incidents and compliance adherence.

Solution: To minimise these risks, enable and centralise logging using tools like AWS CloudTrail, Azure Monitor, or Google Cloud Logging. Ensure logs are stored securely and retained for compliance. Use Security Information and Event Management (SIEM) tools to analyse logs and detect anomalies.

Misconfigurations are preventable with proper planning, regular audits, and the use of cloud-native tools. By addressing common misconfigurations and embedding security into deployment processes, organisations can reduce risks and strengthen their cloud security posture.

COMPLIANCE AND REGULATIONS

Effective cloud security hinges on adherence to regulatory frameworks, ensuring organisations meet legal, ethical, and operational standards. Key regulations such as GDPR, HIPAA, and PCI-DSS demand strong data protection, transparency, and accountability. In cloud environments, compliance is further complicated by data residency, sovereignty concerns, and the shared responsibility model. This chapter delves into the primary compliance challenges, major frameworks, and strategies for meeting regulatory requirements in the cloud. By understanding and addressing these considerations, organisations can mitigate risks, avoid penalties, and cultivate trust within an increasingly regulated digital environment.

WHY COMPLIANCE?

Cloud security compliance is a fundamental aspect of successful cloud adoption. It ensures that organisations meet legal, regulatory, and industry-specific requirements while safeguarding sensitive data and maintaining customer trust. As cloud environments become increasingly complex, adherence to compliance standards is no longer optional but a crucial pillar of cloud adoption.

One of the primary drivers of compliance in the cloud is the need to protect sensitive data, such as personally identifiable information (PII), financial records, or healthcare information. Regulations like the GDPR and HIPAA mandate strict data handling and storage practices. Non-compliance can result in severe penalties, reputational damage, and legal liabilities. By adhering to compliance requirements, organisations ensure that sensitive data is appropriately managed, encrypted, and stored securely, reducing the risk of data breaches.

Customers increasingly demand transparency and assurance that their data is handled responsibly. Demonstrating compliance with standards such as ISO 27001 or SOC 2 shows a continued commitment to security and privacy, building trust and fostering stronger customer relationships. Cloud providers often undergo independent audits to certify their compliance, giving organisations confidence in using their services. However, ultimate responsibility for compliance lies with the customer, especially in respect of the shared responsibility models.

Compliance is often a prerequisite for entering certain markets or industries. For example, organisations dealing with credit card transactions must comply with the Payment Card Industry Data Security Standard (PCI-DSS), while financial institutions may need to adhere to SOX or FFIEC. Failing to meet these requirements can limit business opportunities and disqualify organisations from serving regulated sectors. Cloud compliance ensures market eligibility and enhances competitive advantage.

Non-compliance can lead to financial penalties, legal actions, and operational disruptions. For instance, GDPR fines can reach up to €20 million or 4% of global annual turnover, whichever is higher. Compliance frameworks provide organisations with a structured approach to risk management, helping them identify vulnerabilities and implement safeguards.

Many compliance standards, such as CIS Benchmarks or NIST Cybersecurity Framework, focus on best practices for securing cloud environments. By achieving compliance, organisations enhance their overall security posture, protecting against both regulatory violations and cyber threats.

Compliance is not just about avoiding fines or meeting legal obligations, it is an enabler of trust, security, and business growth. For organisations adopting cloud services, integrating compliance into their business is necessary to ensure resilience, scalability, and long-term business success.

SOC 2, ISO 27001, NIST, GDPR

Organisations leveraging cloud services frequently rely on established frameworks and standards to ensure strong security, operational efficiency, and regulatory compliance. Among the most widely recognized are SOC 2, ISO 27001, NIST, and GDPR, each addressing specific aspects of security and compliance.

SOC 2 is a voluntary framework developed by the American Institute of CPAs (AICPA). It is specifically designed for service providers storing customer data in the cloud, focusing on five trust service criteria: security, availability, processing integrity, confidentiality, and privacy.

• Scope evaluates internal controls to protect customer data.

• Applicability, often required by clients to demonstrate a company's commitment to data security.

• Regular third-party audits ensure adherence.

SOC 2 reports reassure clients that service providers meet industry best practices for data security.

ISO 27001 is a globally recognized standard for Information Security Management Systems (ISMS). It provides a systematic approach to managing sensitive information, including risk assessment, mitigation, and continuous improvement.

• A risk-based approach helps organisations identify and address security risks systematically.

• Certification and independent audits validate compliance.

• Suitable for businesses of all sizes across industries.

ISO 27001 ensures an organisation's security practices are positioned with international standards, promoting trust and confidence.

The NIST Cybersecurity Framework (CSF) provides guidelines to help organisations identify, protect, detect, respond to, and recover from cybersecurity threats. It is widely used in the U.S. and is particularly relevant for federal agencies and their contractors.

It can be tailored to organisations of varying sizes and industries. Consists of five core functions: Identify, Protect, Detect, Respond, Recover. With a strong focus on continuous improvement. NIST CSF is often integrated with other frameworks to enhance cybersecurity resilience.

GDPR is a legal framework established by the European Union to protect personal data and privacy for EU citizens. It applies to any organisation processing EU residents' data, regardless of location.

Covers data collection, processing, storage, and transfer. Includes rights to access, correct, and delete personal data. Non-compliance can result in penalties.

GDPR emphasizes transparency, accountability, and data minimization, making it critical for businesses handling personal data.

SOC 2, ISO 27001, NIST, and GDPR address different aspects of cloud security and compliance, from operational controls to legal requirements. Organisations often adopt multiple frameworks to meet client demands, enhance security, and ensure compliance with international and regional regulations. By positioning with these standards, businesses can build trust, mitigate risks, and achieve long-term success in the cloud.

REGULATORY CHALLENGES

Ensuring compliance in cloud environments is a complex and ongoing process. Organisations must navigate evolving regulations, varying jurisdictional mandates, and the technical intricacies of cloud platforms. The following challenges highlight the difficulties businesses face in ensuring compliance.

Regulations such as GDPR, HIPAA, PCI-DSS, and CCPA differ significantly in scope, requirements, and enforcement. Understanding and implementing controls for multiple standards simultaneously can overwhelm organisations, especially those operating in multiple regions. For example, GDPR focuses on data privacy, while PCI-DSS emphasizes securing payment card information. Positioning these diverse requirements with internal processes requires substantial effort and expertise.

In cloud environments, compliance is as discussed previously, governed by the shared responsibility model, where cloud service providers (CSPs) manage the security of the cloud infrastructure, and customers handle their data and applications. Any misunderstanding of these boundaries can lead to compliance gaps. For instance, an organisation might assume the CSP is responsible for encrypting sensitive data when this falls under the customer's responsibility.

Many regulations impose restrictions on where data can be stored and processed. For instance, GDPR mandates that EU citizens' data must remain within approved regions. Ensuring compliance with these requirements is particularly challenging when leveraging global cloud providers, as data may inadvertently traverse restricted boundaries due to replication or failover mechanisms.

Cloud environments are highly dynamic, with frequent changes in workloads, configurations, and services. This dynamism makes it difficult to maintain compliance, as a single misconfiguration (e.g., opening a storage bucket to the public) can lead to violations. Automated compliance monitoring tools are necessary but often underutilised.

Compliance demands expertise in both regulatory frameworks and cloud technologies. Many organisations lack personnel with this dual skillset, making it difficult to implement and maintain the necessary controls. The shortage of qualified cybersecurity professionals further compounds this issue.

Regulations require regular audits, documentation, and reporting to demonstrate compliance. Manual processes are prone to error and are resource intensive, while automated solutions require proper implementation and maintenance.

As data breaches and cyber threats increase, regulatory bodies frequently update requirements. Organisations must adapt quickly to these changes, which often involve reconfiguring systems, retraining staff, and reassessing risk management practices.

Meeting regulatory requirements in the cloud is a multifaceted challenge requiring technical, operational, and strategic planning. Organisations must invest in skilled personnel, automated tools, and strong compliance processes to navigate these challenges effectively and avoid penalties or reputational damage.

AUTOMATION

Manual compliance reporting in cloud environments is a complex and resource-intensive task. It involves collecting data from various systems, interpreting regulations, and compiling detailed reports. These tasks require significant cross-departmental collaboration and are often subject to errors. In dynamic cloud environments where configurations and workloads change frequently, maintaining accurate and up-to-date records becomes nearly impossible without automation.

Automated compliance tools continuously monitor cloud environments for policy violations and misconfigurations. For instance, they can detect public-facing storage buckets, unauthorised access, or missing encryption in real time, ensuring quick remediation.

Automated tools eliminate human error by standardising the collection and reporting processes. They apply consistent rules and logic, ensuring reports accurately reflect the organisation's compliance status.

As organisations grow and adopt multiple cloud services, automation scales easily to handle the increased complexity. Tools like AWS Config, Azure Policy, or Google Cloud Security Command Centre provide centralised management across multi-cloud environments.

Automated systems generate audit-ready reports, reducing the workload during external assessments. These tools maintain detailed logs, evidence, and documentation required for audits, minimizing disruptions to operations.

Many tools offer pre-built templates for regulations like GDPR, HIPAA, PCI-DSS, and ISO 27001. These templates can be customized to position with specific organisational needs.

Automated tools send real-time alerts when compliance issues arise, enabling rapid responses and minimizing risks.

Centralised dashboards provide visibility into compliance status, highlighting areas requiring attention and facilitating informed decision-making.

Cloud-native tools like AWS Audit Manager, Azure Monitor, and Google Cloud Policy Intelligence are widely used for compliance automation. Third-party platforms such as Tenable, Qualys, and Splunk also integrate consistently with cloud environments to provide enhanced compliance capabilities.

Automation in compliance reporting transforms a traditionally laborious process into an efficient, scalable, and reliable practice. By adopting automated tools, organisations can proactively manage their compliance posture, reduce risks, and ensure readiness for audits, eventually enabling a secure and compliant cloud environment.

CLOUD SECURITY POSTURE MANAGEMENT

Cloud Security Posture Management (CSPM) is a forward-thinking process aimed at detecting and mitigating security threats within cloud environments. As cloud infrastructures become increasingly intricate, CSPM tools offer insights into misconfigurations, compliance shortcomings, and vulnerabilities, ensuring continuous monitoring and automated rectification. This chapter outlines the necessary attributes of CSPM, encompassing real-time threat identification, policy implementation, and consistent integration with DevOps processes. By Utilising CSPM, organisations can remain vigilant against risks, adhere to regulatory requirements, and establish a strong security stance in the ever-evolving threat environment.

INTRODUCTION

Cloud Security Posture Management is a solution designed to enhance security and compliance in cloud environments by identifying and remediating risks associated with misconfigurations, policy violations, and compliance gaps. CSPM tools enable organisations to adopt a proactive security approach, ensuring their cloud infrastructure positions with best practices, regulatory requirements, and organisational policies.

The rapid adoption of cloud services introduces unique security challenges. Unlike traditional on-premises environments, cloud platforms are highly dynamic and decentralised, making them prone to misconfigurations. Common issues such as public-facing storage accounts, overly permissive security group rules, or unencrypted data in transit can lead to data breaches and regulatory penalties.

CSPM addresses these challenges by providing continuous visibility, automated monitoring, and actionable insights to maintain a secure cloud posture.

CSPM tools scan cloud environments to identify misconfigurations and provide recommendations or automated fixes. For instance, they can detect publicly accessible resources or non-compliant encryption settings and suggest corrective actions.

CSPM solutions include pre-built templates for regulatory standards like GDPR, HIPAA, PCI-DSS, and ISO 27001. These templates help organisations ensure their cloud environments adhere to required compliance frameworks, reducing audit burdens.

CSPM tools offer real-time monitoring to detect and alert organisations about risks as they arise, enabling rapid response and minimizing exposure time.

As many organisations operate across multiple cloud providers (e.g., AWS, Azure, and Google Cloud), CSPM tools provide a unified view of security and compliance across these platforms.

CSPM emphasizes proactive security by identifying vulnerabilities before they can be exploited. Unlike reactive security measures that respond to incidents after they occur, CSPM continuously evaluates cloud environments for potential risks. By addressing these risks early, organisations can prevent security breaches, reduce operational disruptions, and maintain trust with customers and stakeholders.

Proactive security through CSPM also includes automation. For example, organisations can configure

CSPM tools to enforce policies automatically, such as denying deployment of unencrypted workloads or revoking excessive permissions.

CSPM is a vital component of modern cloud security. By adopting a proactive approach, organisations can mitigate risks, maintain compliance, and confidently manage their cloud environments in an increasingly complex and interconnected worlds.

DETECTION AND REMEDIATION

CSPM tools are indispensable for maintaining the security and compliance of cloud environments. Their most valuable capabilities include misconfiguration detection and automated remediation, addressing two of the most significant challenges in cloud security.

Misconfigurations are a primary cause of data breaches in cloud environments. These occur when cloud resources are not set up correctly, leaving vulnerabilities that can be exploited. Common examples include public-facing storage accounts, overly permissive IAM roles, unencrypted databases, and insecure network configurations.

CSPM tools excel at detecting such issues by performing extensive scans of cloud environments. These tools continuously evaluate configurations against industry standards, regulatory requirements, and custom policies.

Once misconfigurations are identified, the next step is remediation. Manual remediation can be time-consuming and prone to error, especially in dynamic cloud environments. Automated remediation may address some challenges by enabling tools to fix issues directly or guide teams with actionable recommendations.

TOOLS

To ensure the security and compliance of cloud environments, organisations frequently rely on advanced cloud security tools that offer visibility, policy enforcement, and automated remediation.

AWS Config is an AWS-native service that provides resource configuration management, continuous monitoring, and compliance assessment for AWS environments. AWS Config helps organisations assess, audit, and evaluate the configurations of AWS resources to ensure compliance with internal policies and external regulations.

AWS Config tracks changes to resource configurations, allowing for a complete history of how resources develop over time. It includes pre-built rules for industry standards like PCI-DSS and HIPAA and allows users to create custom rules to evaluate specific configurations. AWS Config enables users to view and analyse configuration changes, providing insights into who made the change and why it occurred. It integrates with AWS CloudTrail, AWS Lambda, and AWS CloudWatch, providing a unified approach to security and compliance monitoring.

AWS Config is particularly useful for organisations that are fully or predominantly on AWS, offering deep integration with AWS services and a strong framework for ensuring continuous compliance and security across all AWS resources.

Azure Security centre is Microsoft Azure's unified security management system, providing advanced threat protection for workloads in the Azure cloud. It integrates with a variety of Azure native services to deliver extensive security monitoring, threat detection, and vulnerability management.

Azure Security centre continuously assesses security configurations and practices to help organisations maintain a secure cloud environment. It detects threats using machine learning, behavioural analytics, and real-time data feeds to identify abnormal activities and potential security incidents. The tool offers built-in regulatory compliance standards such as ISO 27001, GDPR, and NIST, making it easier for businesses to meet regulatory requirements. Azure Security centre integrates with various Azure tools, including Azure Sentinel for SIEM capabilities and Azure Defender for more detailed threat detection.

Azure Security centre offers a strong, extensive security posture management solution specifically for Azure environments. It is well-suited for businesses that use Microsoft's cloud services, offering tools for risk management, regulatory compliance, and threat protection.

ASSESSMENTS AND DEVOPS PIPELINES

Ensuring the security and compliance of a cloud environment necessitates continuous vigilance and proactive measures. Two necessary best practices for maintaining ongoing security and compliance are regular assessments and integrating security into DevOps pipelines. These practices help organisations identify vulnerabilities early, maintain a strong security posture, and embed security into the development lifecycle.

Security is not a one-time task but an ongoing process. Regular assessments are crucial for identifying potential security gaps, misconfigurations, and vulnerabilities in cloud environments. These assessments should be conducted at regular intervals, as well as when there are significant changes to the cloud infrastructure.

Cloud environments are dynamic, with frequent updates, configuration changes, and new deployments. Regular assessments ensure that the environment remains secure and compliant with policies and regulations.

Regular vulnerability scans and configuration checks help detect security issues before they can be exploited by malicious actors. The threat environment is constantly evolving, and new vulnerabilities are discovered regularly. Frequent assessments allow organisations to stay ahead of emerging threats by adjusting security measures in real time.

Using tools like CSPM to detect misconfigurations and ensure adherence to security policies. Periodically conducting penetration tests to simulate attacks and uncover vulnerabilities in cloud applications, networks, and infrastructure.

Reviewing configurations against regulatory frameworks like GDPR, HIPAA, and PCI-DSS to ensure compliance is maintained.

DevOps emphasizes collaboration between development and operations teams to deliver applications quickly and efficiently. However, as development cycles accelerate, security can often become an afterthought. Integrating security into the DevOps pipeline "DevSecOps" ensures that security is considered at every stage of the software development lifecycle (SDLC).

By integrating security early in the development process, organisations can address vulnerabilities before they reach production. This reduces the time and cost associated with fixing security issues later.

By including security testing into CI/CD pipelines, developers can catch vulnerabilities during code commit, build, or deployment. This includes automated scans for vulnerabilities, misconfigurations, and code quality issues.

Once applications are deployed, continuous monitoring ensures that security issues are promptly detected and addressed.

Integrate tools like static application security testing (SAST) and dynamic application security testing (DAST) into the build process to catch security issues early. Implement tools that scan infrastructure as code (IaC) templates for security risks and misconfigurations before deployment.

Educate developers on secure coding practices and encourage them to write code with security in mind. Where possible, set up automatic remediation steps that trigger fixes for minor vulnerabilities or misconfigurations detected during the pipeline process.

Adopting best practices like regular assessments and integrating security into DevOps pipelines ensures that security becomes an integral part of cloud operations and software development. These practices enable organisations to identify and fix issues early, reduce risks, and maintain a strong security posture throughout the lifecycle of their cloud applications and infrastructure. By proactively addressing security concerns, businesses can minimize vulnerabilities, meet compliance requirements, and confidently scale their cloud environments.

MULTI-CLOUD & HYBRID

Managing security across diverse multi-cloud and hybrid environments presents distinct challenges, including maintaining uniformity, managing intricacy, and safeguarding communication across varied platforms. Each cloud provider has its own set of tools and protocols, making integration and visibility necessary for strong security. This chapter delves into best practices for securing these environments, including unified access control, automated compliance checks, and adopting Zero Trust models. With insights into tools and strategies, you will learn how to address the complexities of multi-cloud and hybrid setups, ensuring your organisation can harness their benefits while maintaining a strong and consistent security posture.

CHALLENGES

As businesses seek flexibility, cost optimization, and vendor independence, many adopt multi-cloud or hybrid cloud strategies. While these setups offer benefits like redundancy, performance optimization, and specialized solutions, they also introduce significant challenges, particularly in terms of complexity and consistency.

Managing multiple cloud platforms and integrating on-premises systems with public clouds adds considerable complexity to IT operations.

Each cloud provider (e.g., AWS, Azure, Google Cloud) offers its own set of tools, APIs, and configurations. IT teams must familiarize themselves with different security models, IAM frameworks, and networking setups, leading to a steep learning curve.

Using multiple clouds often requires disparate management tools, making centralised monitoring and control difficult. Security and compliance tools may not provide complete coverage across all platforms, requiring the use of multiple solutions or custom integrations.

Running workloads across multiple environments means maintaining interoperability between systems. Organisations must manage data flows, network connectivity, and application dependencies while ensuring performance and security.

Detecting, analysing, and responding to incidents becomes harder in multi-cloud setups. Logs and telemetry are scattered across platforms, complicating efforts to correlate data and identify root causes.

Achieving consistent policies, processes, and configurations across multiple platforms is one of the biggest hurdles in multi-cloud and hybrid setups.

Ensuring consistent security controls, such as encryption standards, access permissions, and firewall configurations, is challenging when each platform uses different tools and terminology. Mispositioned policies can leave gaps that attackers may exploit.

Different clouds may have different default compliance postures. Ensuring that all environments adhere to frameworks like GDPR, HIPAA, or PCI-DSS requires meticulous effort to position configurations and monitoring practices across platforms.

Applications deployed across multi-cloud or hybrid environments must be designed for portability. Differences in infrastructure (e.g., storage formats or networking capabilities) can lead to performance issues and increased maintenance effort.

Achieving consistent observability across platforms is difficult due to varying logging and monitoring capabilities. Integrating these into a unified dashboard often requires custom development or third-party tools.

1. Leverage multi-cloud management platforms or tools like Kubernetes for orchestration across environments.

2. Use infrastructure as code to enforce consistent configurations and policies.

3. Adopt security tools that provide coverage across clouds, such as CSPM solutions.

4. Automate repetitive tasks like patch management and compliance checks to reduce human error and improve consistency.

While multi-cloud and hybrid setups offer unparalleled flexibility and resilience, they come with significant challenges related to complexity and consistency. Overcoming these requires strategic planning, centralised management, and strong automation to ensure secure, efficient, and consistent operations across all environments.

SECURE COMMUNICATION

As organisations adopt hybrid and multi-cloud strategies, ensuring secure data transmission across diverse environments becomes a critical challenge. This involves managing the complexities of different networking protocols and security mechanisms used by various clouds and on-premises systems. The following challenges must be addressed:

Different clouds and on-premises systems often employ distinct networking protocols and security mechanisms. Managing these variations while ensuring consistent protection can be difficult. Securing communication with encryption and tunnelling may introduce latency, which can affect application performance, particularly in real-time or high throughput use cases.

Tracking data flows across environments becomes harder in hybrid setups, potentially leading to blind spots in security monitoring.

Encryption ensures that data remains confidential as it moves between clouds and on-premises systems. Use TLS (Transport Layer Security) and secure API calls for application communication, and data transfers over the internet. Encrypt traffic between environments for internal communications. Ensure that even intermediary systems cannot access sensitive data by using end-to-end encryption.

Establish a network design that prioritises security and resilience. Connect on-premises data centres to the cloud using site-to-site VPNs for encrypted communication. Utilise dedicated connectivity solutions like AWS Direct Connect or Azure ExpressRoute for high-speed, private communication between clouds and on-premises systems.

Implement zero trust principles by authenticating every data flow and ensuring minimal access privileges. Ensure consistent and secure access between cloud and on-premises systems using federated identity management.

Restrict access to communication endpoints using role-based access controls and the principle of least privilege. Regularly audit and rotate credentials, regularly audit and rotate API keys, certificates, and credentials used for inter-environment communication.

Deploy network monitoring tools to observe traffic patterns and detect anomalies. Use tools to monitor traffic patterns and detect anomalies. Correlate logs from all environments to identify potential threats using SIEM solutions. Enable logging for all communication channels to ensure traceability and facilitate incident response.

Cloud providers offer native tools to simplify and secure hybrid networking, while third-party solutions provide unified management.

Utilise cloud provider native tools like AWS Transit Gateway, Azure Virtual WAN, and Google Cloud Interconnect to simplify and secure hybrid networking.

Securing communication across clouds and on-premises systems requires a layered approach that combines encryption, IAM, secure network architectures, and monitoring. By adopting best practices and leveraging advanced tools, organisations can ensure the confidentiality, integrity, and availability of data as it traverses hybrid and multi-cloud environments.

SECURITY MANAGEMENT TOOLS

In managing intricate cloud and hybrid infrastructures, unified security management tools are indispensable. These tools streamline security operations, ensure consistency, and facilitate scalability.

Terraform for example, enables organisations to define and manage their infrastructure using code, ensuring consistency and repeatability. By leveraging infrastructure as code, teams can incorporate security best practices directly into the deployment process.

Terraform allows users to write infrastructure configurations once and deploy them across multiple environments, ensuring consistent security policies in hybrid and multi-cloud setups. Terraform modules can embed security configurations, such as enforcing encryption for data at rest or enabling security groups, reducing the risk of misconfigurations. Every Terraform plan and apply operation is logged, providing a clear audit trail of infrastructure changes.

Automating the provisioning of firewalls, IAM policies, and network segmentation across cloud platforms. Integrating with compliance tools to ensure configurations meet regulatory standards like SOC 2 or PCI-DSS. Rapidly applying patches to vulnerable infrastructure using predefined templates.

FUTURE TRENDS AND THREATS

Cloud security is undergoing a transformative journey driven by rapid technological advancements and an ever-changing threat environment. Notable innovations such as AI driven threat detection, zero trust architectures, and quantum-resistant encryption are poised to significantly enhance security measures. However, emerging vulnerabilities from quantum computing, edge computing, and increasingly sophisticated AI cyberattacks present substantial challenges.

This chapter delves into these trends and threats, emphasizing the necessity for continuous innovation, collaboration, and agility. By staying informed and proactive, organisations can prepare for the future, ensuring resilient cloud security strategies that adapt to the dynamic digital ecosystem.

AI / ML THREAT DETECTION & ZERO TRUST

The rapid evolution of cloud computing has introduced new security challenges, necessitating advanced technologies to detect and mitigate threats effectively. Two of the most transformative technologies in cloud security are AI/ML in threat detection and Zero Trust models.

Artificial Intelligence (AI) and Machine Learning (ML) are revolutionizing the way threats are identified and addressed in cloud environments.

AI and ML algorithms analyse vast amounts of data in real-time, identifying patterns and anomalies that indicate potential threats. Unlike traditional rule-based systems, AI/ML adapts to new attack vectors, learning from historical data to improve over time.

AI detects deviations from normal behaviour, such as unusual login attempts, sudden data exfiltration, or unauthorised access patterns. Whereas ML models predict potential attack scenarios by analysing historical threat data, enabling proactive defences.

AI-driven systems can trigger automated responses, such as isolating compromised instances or revoking access tokens, to contain threats rapidly. This can lead to faster threat detection and response times. Reduced false positives compared to traditional systems. Scalability to monitor complex, multi-cloud environments.

The Zero Trust model represents a concept shift in cloud security, emphasizing the principle: "Never trust, always verify." This approach assumes that threats can originate both outside and within the network, requiring strict verification for every access request.

Users and systems are granted only the permissions they need to perform specific tasks. Access is continually verified, using factors like location, device health, and user behaviour. Networks are divided into smaller segments to limit lateral movement by attackers.

Services like IAM, MFA, and passwordless authentication are foundational to Zero Trust. They ensure that only secure and trusted devices can access resources. Enforces contextual policies based on the sensitivity of the resource being accessed.

AI/ML and Zero Trust models are reshaping cloud security by addressing modern challenges with intelligence and precision. Together, they allow organisations to detect threats proactively, enforce stringent access controls, and safeguard assets in increasingly complex cloud environments. These technologies represent the future of strong, scalable, and adaptive security.

QUANTUM COMPUTING

As technology advances, so do the risks to cybersecurity. Two emerging areas with significant security implications are quantum computing and edge computing vulnerabilities. While these technologies promise transformative benefits, they also introduce risks that require immediate attention.

Quantum computing, still in its developmental stages, poses a threat to current cryptographic systems. Unlike classical computers, quantum computers Utilise quantum bits, qubits, to perform complex calculations at speeds unattainable by today's standards.

Quantum algorithms, such as Shor's algorithm, can break widely used encryption standards like RSA, ECC, and Diffie-Hellman in a fraction of the time it would take classical computers. This undermines the foundation of secure communications, including SSL/TLS, VPNs, and encrypted emails. Adversaries may already be intercepting and storing encrypted data today, intending to decrypt it when quantum computing becomes practical.

EDUCATION

The rapid evolution of technology presents both opportunities and challenges for cybersecurity professionals. To effectively navigate this dynamic environment, organisations and individuals must adopt a mindset of lifelong learning, ensuring they are prepared for emerging threats and innovative technologies.

Cybersecurity is a field characterized by continuous evolution. New attack methods, vulnerabilities, and technologies arise frequently, necessitating that professionals remain informed and skilled.

Cybersecurity teams must participate in regular training sessions to stay abreast of the latest threats and defensive strategies. Certifications such as CISSP, CEH, and cloud-specific credentials (e.g., AWS Certified Security Specialty) help professionals maintain their expertise.

Utilising threat intelligence platforms keeps teams informed about global cyberattack trends, enabling proactive responses. Labs, simulations, and real-world case studies allow professionals to practice defending against real-time scenarios, enhancing their readiness. As cybersecurity intersects with fields like AI, blockchain, and IoT, understanding these domains enhances the ability to secure diverse environments.

USEFUL RESOURCES

A small collection of resources for continued learning after reading this book. Enjoy!

BOOKS BY AUTHOR

AISec: The Guide to Artificial Intelligence (AI) Solution
Security 2023: AI Security Guide to secure AI solutions
for students, beginners, and cyber security professionals.
Amazon Publishing, 2023

https://www.amazon.co.uk/dp/B0C6XBMVW3

Application Security Essentials: Security Architecture
Series for All Levels. Amazon Publishing, 2023

https://www.amazon.co.uk/dp/B0CFHGV643

Solution Security Essentials: Security Architecture Series for All Levels. Amazon Publishing, 2024

https://www.amazon.co.uk/dp/B0DDBHR4CM

RECOMMENDED BOOKS

Various. *Convergence of Cybersecurity and Cloud Computing.* Pearson, 2024.

Shostack, Adam. *Threat Modeling: Designing for Security.* John Wiley & Sons, 2014.

Jaquith, Andrew. *Security Metrics: Replacing Fear, Uncertainty, and Doubt.* Addison Wesley Professional, 2007

Hubbard W, Douglas. *How to Measure Anything in Cybersecurity Risk.* Wiley, 2023

Magnusson, Andres. *Practical Vulnerability Management: A Strategic Approach to Managing Cyber Risk.* No Starch Press, 2020.

Brikman, Yevgeniy. Terraform – Up and Running: Writing Infrastructure as Code. O'Reilly Media, 2022.

RECOMMENDED TRAINING

• **How to Career Guide into Cyber Security**
https://www.udemy.com/course/how-to-career-guide-into-cyber-security/

Scan the QR code to access all my training and learning resources.

RECOMMENDED ONLINE RESOURCES

- https://csrc.nist.gov

- https://www.cybersecurity-insiders.com/

- https://www.ciat.edu/blog/cloud-security-tools/

- https://owasp.org/www-project-proactive-controls/v3/en/c1-security-requirements

- https://linfordco.com/blog/csa-cloud-controls-matrix/

CONTACTING THE AUTHOR

I can be contacted via LinkedIn, if you have the time, please do take the time to leave a review of this book. It helps to know what was useful and anything to add in future releases. If you have benefitted from the information and if you found it helpful do let me know.

https://www.linkedin.com/in/timcoakley/

Intentionally blank

ABOUT THE AUTHOR

Tim Coakley is a Senior Security Solutions Architect for a large multi-national organisation, an author and creator of numerous cyber security training resources from hands on labs through to specialist courses.

Tim started a long and successful full-time career in Digital Forensics supporting the criminal justice system and law enforcement on a long list of criminal cases. Parallel to this Tim operated a research and development business creating solutions from design through to sales and support resulting in some unique and niche software not developed anywhere else.

Tim now works fully within the cybersecurity space and has supported and worked within many security teams including, Investigations, Incident Response, Threat intelligence, Penetration Testing, Governance and Engineering until landing into Security Architecture.

Cloud Security is a highly sought after profession, with specialist practitioners in this field expected to see significant growth over the coming years. This book provides an extensive overview of the necessary skills and knowledge required in Cloud Security, presented in a concise and accessible manner. Designed for cyber security professionals at all levels and stages of their career, this book draws on extensive experience within the industry.

Tim Coakley
Cybersecurity Professional and Author

Cloud Security Essentials, part of the Security Architecture series, you will learn about:

- What is Cloud Security
- Cloud Identity and Access Management
- Data Encryption in the Cloud
- Cloud Security Audits
- Zero Trust in the Cloud
- Cloud Compliance and Regulations
- Monitoring and Incident Response

www.ingramcontent.com/pod-product-compliance
Lightning Source LLC
LaVergne TN
LVHW051659050326
832903LV00032B/3896